Animal
ABCs

By Susan Hood • Illustrated by Lisa McCue

Troll

Library of Congress Cataloging-in-Publication Data
Hood, Susan.
Animal ABCs / by Susan Hood; illustrated by Lisa McCue.
p. cm.
ISBN 0-8167-3572-7
1. Animals—Juvenile literature.   2. English language—Alphabet—Juvenile
literature.   3. Vocabulary—Juvenile literature.   [1. Animals.   2. Alphabet.
3. Vocabulary.]   I. McCue, Lisa, ill.   II. Title.
QL49.H73   1995   591—dc20 [E]   94-41642

Welcome! Come in and say hello.
The animals want to meet you.
From A to Z, we're all right here,
And waiting in turn to greet you!

A a

A my name is ant.
I know I'm very small.
Tell me, friend, what did you eat
To grow so very tall?

B b

B my name is baby bear.
I love to climb up trees
And hunt for hives of honey.
Watch out! Here come the bees!

C my name is cat.
I have a clever trick.
Instead of using soap to wash,
I lick and lick and lick!

D d

D my name is duckling.
I waddle to and fro.
I follow Mama in a line
Wherever she may go.

E e

E my name is elephant,
And when I cross the trail,
Instead of holding Mama's hand,
I always hold her tail.

F f

F my name is frog.
I croak soft lullabies
To send you gently off to sleep,
As stars light up the skies.

G g

G my name is gander.
My wife and I are geese.
With all our growing goslings,
There's never any peace!

Hh

H my name is hippo.
I love to take my bath.
I scrub-a-dub with lovely mud
And make hyena laugh!

Ii

I my name is ibex.
My hooves have quite a grip.
I run straight up the mountainside
Where others sometimes slip.

J j

J my name is jaguar.
And though I'm polka-dotted,
In among the jungle trees,
I'm hardly ever spotted.

Kk

K my name is kangaroo.
I have a pocket, too,
But mine is not
for keys and such.
It's just for you-know-who!

L my name is lion.
I lie in the sun all day.
When I yawn, I wonder why
The others run away.

M m

M my name is monkey.
These vines are my trapeze.
Come watch me swing and somersault
And dangle from my knees.

N n

N my name is narwhal.
My tooth looks like a horn.
Perhaps that's why some call me
A deep-sea unicorn.

Oo

O my name is octopus.
Just think what you could do
If you had eight arms
    just like me
Instead of only two!

P p

P my name is piglet
And I am getting big.
Mama smiles and likes to say
I eat just like a pig!

Q q

Q my name is quail.
I'm quite a handsome chap,
A jaunty, dashing fellow
With a feather in my cap.

R r

R my name is rabbit.
My burrow's underground.
I dug this cozy bunny bed
To keep us safe and sound.

S s

S my name is sheep.
I have a woolly sweater.
I wear it morning, noon, and night,
In every kind of weather.

T t

T my name is turtle.
I'm never far from home.
I tuck myself in my own bed
No matter where I roam.

U u

U my name is unicorn.
Come chase me, my young friend.
You'll only catch me in your dreams,
For I am just pretend!

V v

V my name is vulture.
Some people call me vile,
But that must surely be because
They've never seen me smile!

Ww

W my name is whale.
I sing beneath the sea.
My song is heard for miles around
And echoes back to me.

Xx   Yy

X my name is xenops.
Come meet my friend, the yak.
A better friend there never was—
I ride him piggyback!

Z my name is zebra.
My stripes are black as night.
Or is it that my back is black,
And all my stripes are white?

It's time to say, "Good-bye! So long!
Farewell, friend! Toodle-loo!"
But just before you close this book,
Please tell us your name, too!